D1162223

Revised and Updated

Heinemann
STATE
STUDIES

People of Texas

Mary Dodson Wade

Heinemann Library
Chicago, Illinois

© 2004, 2008 Heinemann Library
a division of Reed Elsevier Inc.
Chicago, Illinois

Customer Service 888-454-2279

Visit our website at **www.heinemannlibrary.com**

All rights reserved. No part of this publication may be reproduced or transmitted in any form or by any means, electronic or mechanical, including photocopying, recording, taping, or any information storage and retrieval system, without permission in writing from the publisher.

Designed by Kimberly R. Miracle and Betsy Wernert
Photo Research by Tracy Cummins
Printed and bound in China by Leo Paper Group Ltd

12 11 10 09 08
10 9 8 7 6 5 4 3 2 1

New edition ISBNs: 978-1-4329-1154-6 (hardcover)
                   978-1-4329-1161-4 (paperback)

The Library of Congress has cataloged the first edition as follows:
Wade, Mary Dodson.
  People of Texas / Mary Dodson Wade.
     v. cm. -- (Heinemann state studies)
Includes bibliographical references and index.
Contents: Texas's people -- First people and early settlers --
Immigration to Texas -- Texas's achievers.
  ISBN 1-4034-0689-8 -- ISBN 1-4034-2695-3
  1. Ethnology--Texas--Juvenile literature. 2.
Minorities--Texas--Juvenile literature. 3. Immigrants--Texas--Juvenile literature.
4. Texas--Population--Juvenile literature. 5. Texas--History--Juvenile literature.
6. Texas--Biography--Juvenile
literature. [1. Texas--Population. 2. Immigrants--Texas.] I. Title. II. Series.
  F395.A1W33 2003
  305.8'009764--dc21
                        2003009547

Acknowledgments
The author and publishers are grateful to the following for permission to reproduce copyright material:

Cover photograph reproduced with permission of ©Getty Images/Glowimages

pp. 4, 20, 24 Bob Daemmrich/The Image Works; **p. 11t** Center for American History, UT-Austin; **pp. 11b, 26t, 34** The Granger Collection, NY; **p. 12** Hulton Archive/Getty Images; **p. 13** Friends of the Governor's Mansion, Austin, TX; **pp. 14, 35** Bettmann/Corbis; **p. 15** Joe Sohm/The Image Works; **p. 17t** Park Street/PhotoEdit; **p. 17b** XIT Ranch Museum/AP Wide World Photo; **p. 18** Library of Congress; **p. 19** Robert Brenner/Photo Edit; **p. 21** Courtesy of the Witte Museum, San Antonio, Texas; **p. 22t** Texas Parks and Wildlife Department; **p. 22b** E. R. N. Reed; **p. 23** Kathleen Leininger; **p. 25** Jim Gramon; **pp. 26b, 29b, 38b** Brown Brothers; **pp. 27, 29t** John Troesser, editor/TexasEscapes.com; **p. 28** Holocaust Museum Houston; **p. 30** Jim Olive/Stockyard.com; **p. 31** Bob Daemmrich/Photo Edit; **pp. 32, 38t, 39, 42** AP Wide World Photo; **p. 33** Gerald Herbert/AP Photo; **pp. 36, 41** Corbis; **p. 37** Texas Energy Museum/AP Wide World Photo; **p. 40** National Cowgirl Museum and Hall of Fame/Fort Worth, Texas; **p. 43t** Library of Congress prints and photographs; **p. 43b** Amanda Edwards/Getty Images; **p. 44** Texas State Library and Archives Commission

Every effort has been made to contact copyright holders of any material reproduced in this book. Any omissions will be rectified in subsequent printings if notice is given to the publisher.

Disclaimer
All the Internet addresses (URLs) given in this book were valid at the time of going to press. However, due to the dynamic nature of the Internet, some addresses may have changed, or sites may have changed or ceased to exist since publication. While the author and publisher regret any inconvenience this may cause readers, no responsibility for any such changes can be accepted by either the author or the publisher.

Contents

Some words are shown in bold, **like this**. You can find out what they mean by looking in the glossary.

Many Texans

Texas is larger than any other state in the United States except Alaska. It is not surprising that it ranks second in population of all 50 states. Only California has more people. Texans today come from many different **ethnic** backgrounds, making Texas one of the most **diverse** states in the nation.

The 2000 Census

The population of Texas has increased greatly over the years. In 1900 the population was just over 3 million. According to the 2000 **census**, almost 21 million people were living in Texas. A huge increase in population occurred between 1990 and 2000. About one of every four people living in Texas came to the state during that time. As of 2006, it was estimated that close to 23.5 million people were living in the state.

Although **Anglos** were the first people to settle in Texas, the state now is home to people of every race and ethnicity.

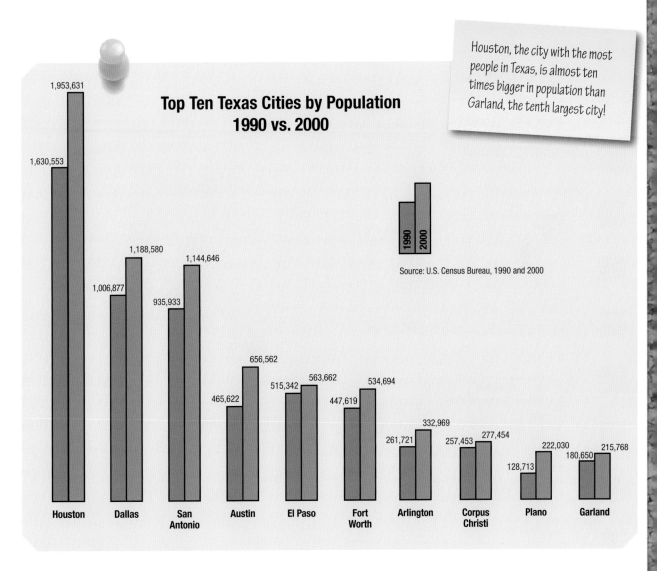

Top Ten Texas Cities by Population
1990 vs. 2000

Houston: 1,630,553 (1990), 1,953,631 (2000)
Dallas: 1,006,877 (1990), 1,188,580 (2000)
San Antonio: 935,933 (1990), 1,144,646 (2000)
Austin: 465,622 (1990), 656,562 (2000)
El Paso: 515,342 (1990), 563,662 (2000)
Fort Worth: 447,619 (1990), 534,694 (2000)
Arlington: 261,721 (1990), 332,969 (2000)
Corpus Christi: 257,453 (1990), 277,454 (2000)
Plano: 128,713 (1990), 222,030 (2000)
Garland: 180,650 (1990), 215,768 (2000)

1990 | 2000

Source: U.S. Census Bureau, 1990 and 2000

Houston, the city with the most people in Texas, is almost ten times bigger in population than Garland, the tenth largest city!

There are 5,800 cities and towns in Texas. They range in population from under 50 people to almost 2 million. Texas has 24 cities with more than 100,000 people. Houston is the largest city, with a population of almost 2 million in 2000. Dallas, San Antonio, Austin, and El Paso follow in population size. Houston, Dallas, and San Antonio are also among the ten most populated cities in the United States.

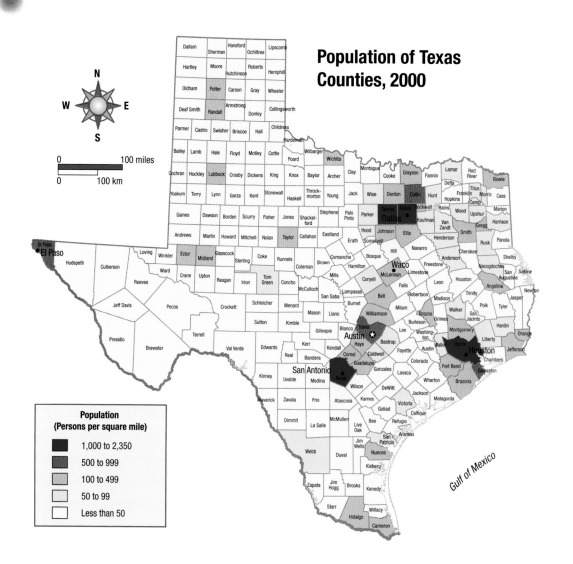

Population of Texas Counties, 2000

N W E S

0 — 100 miles
0 — 100 km

Population
(Persons per square mile)

- 1,000 to 2,350
- 500 to 999
- 100 to 499
- 50 to 99
- Less than 50

Gulf of Mexico

Where People in Texas Live

In 1910 about 75 percent of the people in Texas lived in **rural** areas. Only 20 percent live in rural areas today. About 80 percent of the people in the state live in **urban** areas. This means that out of every 100 people who live in Texas, 80 live in one of the state's cities.

The population is highest in areas where there are large cities, such as Dallas, San Antonio, and Houston. The communities around these cities are highly populated as well.

Most Texans live in the state's **metropolitan** areas. These areas include Austin-San Marcos, Dallas, **Fort** Worth-Arlington, Houston, and San Antonio. The change from rural to urban areas mainly happened because people began using machines to do farm work. As a result, many people left the farms to find work in the growing **industries** in the cities.

A Diverse State

Texas's people represent many races and ethnicities. About 83 percent of Texans are Caucasian, and almost 12 percent are African American. Other peoples, such as Asians and Native Americans, make up a very small percentage of the entire population—about 3 percent.

About a third of the people of Texas are of **Hispanic descent**. Most Hispanic people in Texas are Mexican Americans. Other groups of Texans have German, Italian, and Czech backgrounds. Texas's different **cultural** groups make the state one of the most diverse states in the nation.

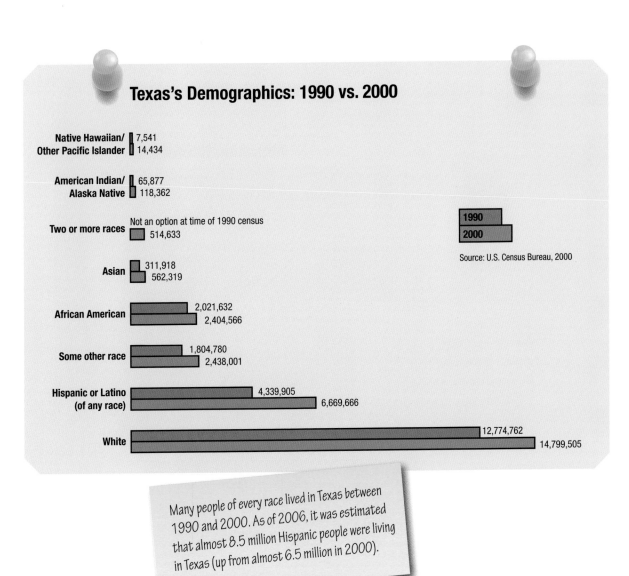

Texas's Demographics: 1990 vs. 2000

	1990	2000
Native Hawaiian/Other Pacific Islander	7,541	14,434
American Indian/Alaska Native	65,877	118,362
Two or more races	Not an option at time of 1990 census	514,633
Asian	311,918	562,319
African American	2,021,632	2,404,566
Some other race	1,804,780	2,438,001
Hispanic or Latino (of any race)	4,339,905	6,669,666
White	12,774,762	14,799,505

Source: U.S. Census Bureau, 2000

Many people of every race lived in Texas between 1990 and 2000. As of 2006, it was estimated that almost 8.5 million Hispanic people were living in Texas (up from almost 6.5 million in 2000).

First People and Early Settlers

The first people to come to the present-day United States **migrated** from Asia to North America, beginning about 14,000 years ago. It is believed that these people migrated over a land bridge that connected Asia with North America. Today, that land bridge is covered by water and called the Bering Strait.

Paleo-Indians

The first group of people to arrive in the area that is now Texas were the Paleo-Indians. They developed a **culture** based on the **environment**. They lived in rock shelters near Del Rio, gathered plants and berries, and hunted small animals. Paleo-Indians also lived along the Rio Grande, in the Panhandle, and in central Texas.

Migration Routes

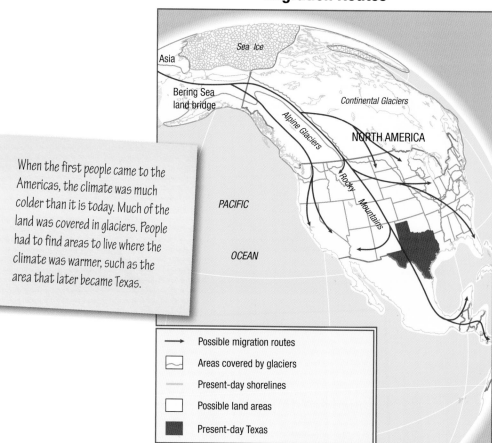

When the first people came to the Americas, the climate was much colder than it is today. Much of the land was covered in glaciers. People had to find areas to live where the climate was warmer, such as the area that later became Texas.

→ Possible migration routes

☐ Areas covered by glaciers

— Present-day shorelines

☐ Possible land areas

■ Present-day Texas

Texas's First Native Tribes

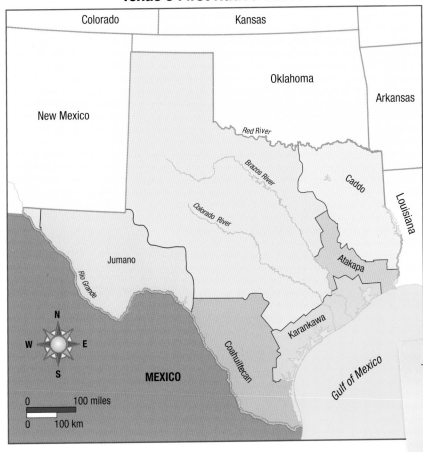

This map shows the general location of the first tribes of Texas. However, the tribes moved around to hunt and trade and they did not keep to exact borders.

Native Americans

Texas was home to tribes, bands, and groups of Native Americans who lived in all areas of the state. The actual number of Native Americans in the state is not known, especially because they often moved from place to place and did not always name themselves. The names we know them by were given to them by others.

The first written records mentioning Native Americans began in the 1500s, at the time of the arrival of European explorers and settlers. The first records included tribes along the coast, where the explorers landed. These records included descriptions of the Native American tribes in Texas, such as the Caddo, Atakapa, Coahuiltecan, Karankawa, and Jumano. Later, as more settlers began moving west, new groups of Native Americans moved into Texas. The Wichita, Apache, Tonkawa, Kiowa, Kiowa Apache, Comanche, Cherokee, and Choctaw all found places to settle here.

Moving To Reservations

By the early 1800s, the U.S. government forced many Native Americans from their lands in the eastern part of the United States. Then, in 1839, the U.S. government ordered all Native Americans to leave the Republic of Texas. Many went to the Indian Territory, which is now Oklahoma. Only the Alabama and the Coushatta were allowed to stay in East Texas. Today, the Tigua, the Alabama-Coushatta, and a small group of Kickapoo live on **reservations** in the state.

Indian Reservations in Texas

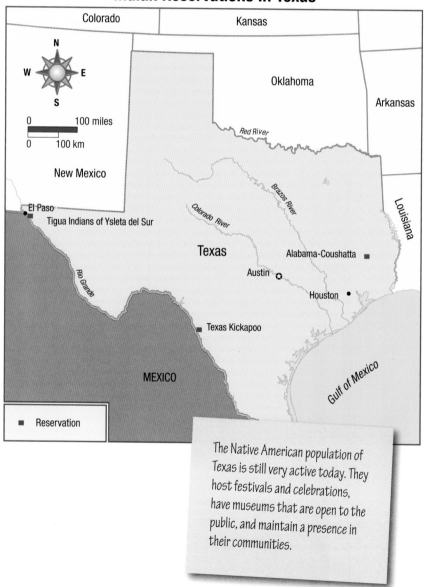

The Native American population of Texas is still very active today. They host festivals and celebrations, have museums that are open to the public, and maintain a presence in their communities.

In central Texas, many Native American tribes lived in small communities and on farms, traveling only when necessary. It was not always safe to travel.

Spanish Explorers Arrive in Texas

The Spanish first landed in Texas in 1528. These people were part of an **expedition** that was shipwrecked off the Texas coast. Álvar Núñez Cabeza de Vaca and several followers traveled among the Native Americans there.

When Cabeza de Vaca reported his findings to the king of Spain, the report was not entirely true. A slave added to the story by saying the group had found "Seven Golden Cities of Cibola," where people lived a life of luxury. The Spanish king heard these stories, and sent expeditions to find these cities. In 1541, Hernando de Soto, a Spanish adventurer, explored East Texas. At the same time, Francisco Vásquez de Coronado, another explorer, marched across the Texas Panhandle. Of course, these golden cities did not exist. Spain claimed all the land around the Gulf of Mexico.

Álvar Núñez Cabeza de Vaca was the first European merchant in Texas. He traveled around Texas, trading beans and seashells for furs and red iron ore.

Spain also set up **missions** here. The Spanish missions in Texas were established to spread Christianity, especially among the Native Americans. The first two missions were started in 1682. They were located near what is now the city of El Paso. In 1718 Spain established Mission San Antonio de Valero, which became known as the Alamo. They also built a military post there to protect it from the Native Americans, who were upset that the Spanish were invading their lands. By the late 1700s, the Spanish had settled in what are now the cities of San Antonio, Laredo, Nacogdoches, and Goliad.

How Texas Got Its Name

The early Spanish settlers called a group of Caddo Indians the Tejas. *Tejas* was that group's word for "friend." The Mexicans who would later live there used the word when referring to the region. Eventually, the word became *Texas*, the state name.

In 1821 Mexico became independent of Spain, and the land that is now Texas became a part of Mexico. In January 1821, an American named Moses Austin came to San Antonio from Missouri to ask Mexico's permission to bring American settlers into Texas. Moses Austin died five months later, and his son, Stephen Fuller Austin, completed a settlement contract with the new Mexican government.

Mexico also developed the *empresario* system to attract even more people to Texas. By 1836, 35,000 people lived in the area.

Hernando de Soto encouraged his men to keep moving by promising that gold was "just ahead."

The Battle of the Alamo occurred on March 6, 1839, after 13 days of holding off Mexican soldiers. Approximately 189 men died during the fight.

As more people came to Texas, the Mexican government became concerned that the United States government wanted the land for its country. The Mexican congress passed the Decree of April 6, 1830 that said that no more Americans could enter Texas. Agreements with *empresarios* who did not cooperate were canceled. A tax on goods coming from the United States made trade impossible. These new laws upset the settlers. They created a state constitution made up of their own laws for the area, but it was rejected by the Mexican government. The Texas Revolution began in October 1835.

Sam Houston, James Bowie, William Travis, and David "Davy" Crockett all had large roles in the Texas Revolution. Houston, the **commander** of the Texas army, sent Bowie with a small force to San Antonio in January 1836. Travis arrived with soldiers on February 3. Five days later, Crockett rode into San Antonio with a dozen fighters from Tennessee. Travis and Bowie shared command of the 180 men gathered there. During the Battle of the Alamo, Crockett, Travis, and Bowie all lost their lives. The fighting for Texas's independence continued until April, when Mexican forces were defeated at the Battle of San Jacinto. Texas then became an independent republic.

Four presidents served the Republic of Texas from 1836 to 1846: Sam Houston, Mirabeau Lamar, David Burnet, and Anson Jones. All four men struggled with making and maintaining peace with both the Native American groups of Texas and their Mexican neighbors to the south. It was during Jones's term that Mexico finally accepted Texas's independence. Jones gave Texans the choice of whether to remain an independent republic or join the United States. The people chose to become part of the United States. On December 29, 1845, President James K. Polk signed the act that made Texas the 28th state.

Reminders of Texas's Past

Although Texas has been a state for over 150 years, the Spanish influence in Texas can still be seen today. Forty-one counties and many Texas towns have Spanish names. The squares that can be found in the center of some Texas towns and cities were influenced by Spanish plazas. Spanish influence can also be seen in the state's architecture, music, and food.

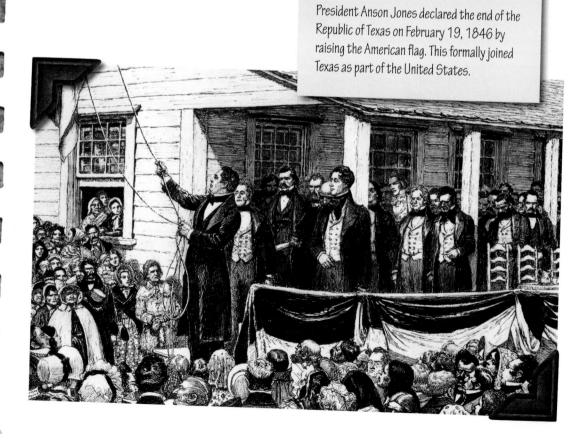

President Anson Jones declared the end of the Republic of Texas on February 19, 1846 by raising the American flag. This formally joined Texas as part of the United States.

Cultural Groups in Texas

Mariachi groups are popular entertainment at restaurants, parties, weddings, and other occasions.

People of all races, **ethnicities**, and **heritages** live in Texas. Each different group has contributed to the state through art, music, architecture, food, and more.

Mexicans

Texans of Mexican **descent** are often called Tejanos. Tejanos played an important role in Texas history. They fought for Texas's independence from Mexico. José Francisco Ruiz and his nephew, José Antonio Navarra, were the only two people born in Texas who signed the Texas Declaration of Independence. Gregorio Esparza was one of the seven Tejano defenders inside the Alamo during a battle against Mexico. Once Texas became independent of Mexico, Tejano communities were found in Nacogdoches, San Antonio, Goliad, and Laredo, though many Tejanos returned to Mexico. Tejano communities combined both Mexican traditions with American **culture**. These communities maintained their religious beliefs, celebrated Mexican holidays, and spoke Spanish, but as more children were born, the culture shifted to more American ways of life.

In the 1920s, many Tejanos fled to Texas to escape the Mexican Revolution (1910–1920). They took jobs on the newly established farms in South Texas. However, racial violence often occurred, with many people killed or wounded. Mexican Americans fought **discrimination** and poor treatment by joining labor unions and other organizations. Tejanos also were denied the right to vote, to serve on juries, and to attend good schools. Several Tejano groups were formed to fight these problems, including the League of United Latin American Citizens (LULAC) and the American G.I. Forum. The work of these groups changed the way Tejanos were viewed by the **Anglo** people, though there are still struggles for equality today.

Mexican influences can still be seen in Texas today. *Mariachi* bands play lively tunes. Conjunto music, which features accordions, is a mixture of Mexican folk songs and Czech and German polkas. Piñatas are broken at children's parties. Charro Days is Brownsville's version of a rodeo. Fiesta San Antonio began as the Battle of the Flowers, a yearly event to honor those who died in the Battle of the Alamo and the Battle of San Jacinto. It has now become a ten-day celebration of all cultures in Texas.

Anglos

In the early 1800s, before Texas was part of the United States, the Spanish officials allowed people from the United States to enter Texas. In 1820 Moses Austin, a Missouri banker, received permission from the Spanish to set up a colony in Texas. However, he died before he could do so. His son, Stephen Fuller Austin, carried out the plan and brought 300 families to start a colony in southeast Texas. Mexico soon issued more land grants to start colonies. The Mexicans called these people *empresarios*. They called the settlers Anglos because almost all had British or Northern European **ancestors**. These settlers brought a new language, laws, and customs to Texas.

When the first Anglos arrived, Texas had fewer than 4,000 people living in three towns. About 15,000 Native Americans lived in unsettled areas. Fifteen years later, there were 35,000 settlers, most from other parts of the United States.

British

The British did not establish any major settlements in Texas. However, British people did settle all over the state. Several English citizens **invested** in West Texas ranches. A British group called The Capitol Freehold Land & Investment Company built the XIT ranch on 3 million acres (1.2 million hectares) of land. The company received the land in exchange for money to build the state **capitol**. The largest number of British **immigrants** came to Texas in the 1940s, after the end of World War II. These immigrants were the wives of U.S. soldiers who were returning home to Texas after the war.

Although this monument to Moses Austin stands in San Antonio, his remains are buried in Missouri. There have been several unsuccessful attempts to bring him back to Texas to be buried in the State Cemetery.

The XIT ranch was intended as a new way of raising cattle by keeping them in a closed-off area instead of raising them on the open range.

Today, Texans celebrate their British heritage with annual costumed festivals. These include Dickens on the Strand in Galveston, Scarborough Faire in Waxahachie, and the Texas Renaissance Festival in Plantersville.

African Americans

About 12 percent of Texans in 2000 were African Americans. Africans arrived in Texas with the first Europeans in the 1500s. After Texas was opened for settlement, slaveholders brought slaves to Texas to work cotton and sugar **plantations**.

Most slaves had food, clothing, and a crude log cabin for shelter, but they also worked as field hands from sunrise to sunset.

As more cotton was produced, the number of slaves in Texas grew. By 1860, the number reached 182,000—almost one third of the state's population. Then on June 19, 1865, General Gordon Granger arrived in Galveston to announce freedom for slaves. He was there to enforce the **Emancipation Proclamation** after the end of the Civil War (1861–1865). The Juneteenth holiday celebrates that day. Some former slaves became **sharecroppers**, paying part of their crops as rent. Kendleton was founded when sharecroppers bought land from William E. Kendall in the 1860s.

Juneteenth celebrations are marked by parades, guest speakers, picnics, and family gatherings.

Although they were free after the Civil War, African Americans continued to experience discrimination. Laws **segregated** them in schools, transportation, and other public places. African Americans worked to gain equal rights. Finally, in the 1950s and 1960s, laws were passed that made segregation illegal. Many African Americans began to run for political office. In 1972 Barbara Jordan was elected to the **House of Representatives**. She was the first African American in Texas history to represent Texas in **Congress**.

African Americans also contributed to Texas's heritage in other ways. Musicians such as Blind Lemon Jefferson, Huddie Ledbetter, Eddie Durham, Scott Joplin, and Bobbi Humphrey created new sounds in blues, jazz, and ragtime. Artist John Biggers of Houston became one of the nation's most important mural painters and an internationally recognized artist. In sports, Charlie Taylor, Ernie Banks, Jack Johnson, and George Foreman earned national fame in football, baseball, and boxing.

Immigration to Texas

The population of Texas grew rapidly in the 1800s. A major reason for the increase in population was immigration. People came to Texas for several reasons. Some came in search of land because of a shortage of land in their own countries. Some came to escape governments they did not like. Others came to escape poverty and overcrowding. Whatever the reason, these **immigrants** helped to make Texas a **diverse** state.

Germans

Germans were the largest group of European immigrants to come to Texas. German immigration began in the 1830s and increased after the Civil War ended in 1865. Many Germans immigrated from Germany because they did not like their government. They settled in what is now New Braunfels, Comfort, and Fredericksburg. The Society for the Protection of German Immigrants brought 7,000 immigrants to Texas in the mid-1840s. John O. Meusebach led

The Wurstfest Opa Band plays every year at the Folklife Festival held at the Institute of Texan Cultures in San Antonio.

a group of professionals and farmers who made a **treaty** with the Comanche. He promised the Comanche gifts worth $1,000 in return for their pledge not to disturb or harm the colonists. In May 1847, the Comanche chiefs came to Fredericksburg to sign the Meusebach-Comanche Treaty and collect their gifts.

Easter Fires in Fredericksburg

On the night before Easter each year, a Fredericksburg pageant celebrates the town's treaty with the Comanche. The story says that children were frightened by signal fires but their mothers told them it was the Easter Rabbit dyeing eggs. True story or not, the treaty hangs in the Texas State Archives. In 1996 a group of Comanche came from Oklahoma to be part of Fredericksburg's 150th anniversary celebration.

The Germans made many contributions to Texas's **culture**. Germans built stone houses, some of which still stand in Texas today. They were known for music and dancing. They formed athletic clubs and groups that held singing festivals. Artist Hermann Lundquist painted landscapes. His brother-in-law, Richard Petri, created paintings of Native Americans. Ferdinand Lindheimer has been called the Father of Texas Botany because he identified and classified Texas plants. Inventor Jacob Brodbeck built an airplane that flew briefly, 40 years before the famous Wright brothers' plane.

Richard Petri's paintings were respected for their accurate reflection of Native American life.

The Germans became proud Americans. Round Top has held a Fourth of July parade every year since 1852, even during the Civil War. German Texans did not support slavery. A group of German men left for Mexico in 1862 to avoid joining the **Confederate** army. They were killed near the Nueces River. Their remains were buried in Comfort under a monument that reads "Treue der Union" which means "True to the Union." Germans also preserve their **heritage** with German Texan societies. Even today, German is spoken in some of the communities.

With the exception of those in national cemeteries, this is believed to be the only monument honoring the Union in a former Confederate state.

Fleet Admiral Chester W. Nimitz is honored in the Admiral Nimitz State Historic site in Fredericksburg, Texas.

During World War II (1939–1945), the **commander** of the United States Pacific fleet was Admiral Chester William Nimitz of Fredericksburg, Texas. He was a grandson of one of the original German settlers of Fredericksburg. The building and grounds of his grandfather's hotel in Fredericksburg contain a museum about World War II.

Czechs

Czechs were the second largest European group to immigrate from Europe. They came from the present-day countries of Slovakia and the Czech Republic. They settled in Cat Spring, New Ulm, Fayetteville, and Praha. About 700 Czechs were living in Texas by 1860. By 1920, the number reached about 15,000. Most Czech immigrants were farmers who came to Texas for better opportunities and to escape political problems in their country. They grew most of the food they needed but sold corn for money. It was a tradition that before a Czech couple married, they had to own or rent land to farm.

Some Czechs were protestants called Moravians. Others were **Catholics** who built beautiful painted churches found in Fayette County. The Czechs worked to preserve their language by publishing newspapers in their language. The Czech Museum is located in Temple, Texas.

Elisabet Ney Sculptures

Every state in the U.S. has sent statues of two outstanding citizens to be part of Statuary Hall in Washington, D.C. For Texas, sculptor Elisabet Ney, who was born in Germany, created statues of Stephen Austin and Sam Houston. Duplicates are at the state **capitol** building in Austin, Texas.

In 1984, 15 of these painted churches were listed on the National Register of Historic Places.

A Czech organization in Texas that helps to preserve Czech culture is the Sokol, which is Czech for *falcon*. Sokol's motto is "a sound mind in a sound body." The organization combines programs that help develop the mind as well as those that develop the body. Sokol is especially known for its gymnastic programs.

Kolaches

Kolaches are small pastries filled with poppy seeds, fruit, or sometimes meat. Czech women have no recipe for the kolache dough—they just show the next generation how to make it.

A popular Czech saying is, "Every Czech is born with a violin under his pillow." Instruments of all types are featured at the National Polka Festival held in Ennis each year. Czech Days held in Rosenberg and the Kolache Festival held in Halletsville also help preserve Czech culture in Texas today.

Irish

The Irish were in Texas long before the **Anglos** arrived. Two *empresario* grants went to Irishmen. John McMullen and his son-in-law James McGloin named their area San Patricio in honor of St. Patrick. Their settlers were Irish immigrants who came from New York City in 1829. James Power and James Hewetson went to Ireland in 1833 to bring back colonists. They settled around Refugio. By 1850, there were 1,403 Irish in Texas, and that number reached 3,480 by 1860. Many Irish immigrated to Texas to escape **famine** in Ireland.

Bishop's Palace in Galveston was constructed in 1886 for $250,000. It is ranked among the top 100 homes in the nation for its architectural importance.

Every year, floats release 35 pounds (16 kilograms) of **environmentally**-friendly green dye into the San Antonio River. A proclamation is read, temporarily renaming the river The River Shannon, just like the one in Ireland.

During the 1800s, Irish cowboys worked on cattle ranches. Irish workers helped to build the railroads in Texas. John Shearn helped to make Houston an important port city. Nicholas J. Clayton designed the Bishop's Palace in Galveston.

Today, towns such as Shamrock and Dublin hold annual St. Patrick's Day events. New generations of Irish Texans learn fast-stepping Irish dances. San Antonio helps honor Irish culture by dyeing the water along the Riverwalk green on St. Patrick's Day.

Scandinavians

Some Texans are **descendants** of people from the countries of Scandinavia—Denmark, Sweden, and Norway. The largest number of Danes immigrated to Texas between 1885 and 1895.

The first group of Swedish immigrants arrived in Texas in 1838. More Swedes arrived in Texas between 1848 and 1910. By 1900, there were about 4,000 Swedish settlers in Texas. At first, most Swedish settlements were **rural**. Later, many Swedes settled near Austin, Dallas, and other smaller towns. The city names of Lund, New Sweden, and Swensondale show the Swedish influence. Today, about 160,000 Texans are of Swedish **descent**.

A large group of Norwegians settled in Bosque County, west of Waco, around 1854. Johan Reinert Reiersen had written home to urge Norwegians to move to Texas. His father Ole bought land in Henderson County and founded Brownsboro.

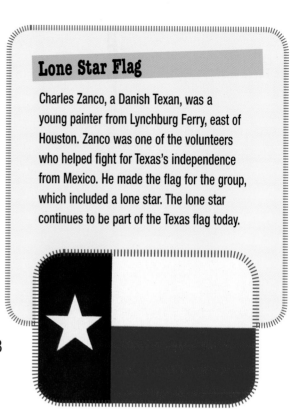

Lone Star Flag

Charles Zanco, a Danish Texan, was a young painter from Lynchburg Ferry, east of Houston. Zanco was one of the volunteers who helped fight for Texas's independence from Mexico. He made the flag for the group, which included a lone star. The lone star continues to be part of the Texas flag today.

Mildred "Babe" Didriksen Zaharias

Mildred Didriksen, a Norwegian Texan, was born in Port Arthur in 1911. Her ability to hit a baseball like Babe Ruth led to her nickname. She has been called the greatest woman athlete of all time. She excelled in every sport and dominated women's events in the 1932 Olympics. She later married George Zaharias and became a famous golfer. The Babe Didriksen Museum is in Beaumont.

Italians

The largest number of Italian immigrants came to Texas between 1880 and 1920. Most came to make a better life for themselves and their families. Many Italians settled in the Brazos River valley. They worked as farmers, miners, or factory workers. Around League City and Dickinson, Italians raised figs and strawberries. At Del Rio they planted vineyards and established wineries. Italians also mined coal and made bricks in Thurber, a town that no longer exists.

Several Italians left creative marks on Texas. Sculptor Pompeo Coppini created many statues that can be seen throughout the state. **Architects** Oscar and Frederick Ruffini designed many Texas courthouses.

Italian festivals center around the church. Loaves of bread fill altars on St. Joseph's Day, March 19. The city of Keller holds Festival Italiano each year around Columbus Day in October.

In 1945 Coppini cofounded the Classic Arts Fraternity in San Antonio. It was renamed Coppini Academy of Fine Arts in 1950.

The Holocaust Museum Houston has a permanent exhibit that focuses on Houston-area Holocaust survivors.

Jews

Jewish people came to Texas from different countries. Many immigrated to escape **persecution** in Eastern Europe. By 1920, about 30,000 Jews had settled in Texas. Many settled in Texas's major cities, such as Dallas, Houston, and **Fort** Worth. After World War II, the number of Jews in Texas increased from 50,000 in 1945 to about 71,000 in the mid-1970s. Like earlier Jewish immigrants, they also settled in large **urban** areas.

Jewish leaders have supported Texas orchestras, museums, hospitals, and libraries. The Holocaust Museum Houston in Houston and the Dallas Memorial Center for Holocaust Studies honor millions of Jews killed during World War II.

Polish

Panna Maria, near San Antonio, is thought to be the oldest permanent Polish settlement in the nation. One hundred families came when Father Leopold Moczygemba, a young priest in Castroville, Texas, wrote letters home about the state. Father Moczygemba is buried in Panna Maria under the live oak tree where he held the first church service on Christmas Day 1854.

New Polish communities started near Panna Maria. They included Falls City, Kosciusko, and Karnes City in southern Texas. Poles also settled in communities near Houston and Austin.

Father Moczygemba purchased 238 acres (96 hectares) near Panna Maria. He set aside land for a church and divided the remaining land among those who could not afford to buy farms.

Chinese

The first Chinese immigrants to Texas were single men who built railroads. Hundreds of them worked on a railroad line from Dallas to Houston in the 1870s. Some stayed in Robertson County as farm workers. Ten years later, the Southern Pacific Railroad had 2,600 Chinese workers building eastward from El Paso. At the same time, Irish workers for the Texas and Pacific Railroad worked westward from central Texas. On January 12, 1883, the two lines met at the Pecos River in Val Verde County. Railroad owners drove a silver spike to complete the nation's second **transcontinental** railroad.

Pancho Villa, a Mexican **revolutionary**, helped bring Chinese workers to Texas. In 1917 U.S. General John J. Pershing made an unsuccessful trip into Mexico to capture Villa. Chinese people were living in northern Mexico, hoping to enter the United States. They cooked and did laundry for Pershing's troops. Four hundred of them followed the general back to **Fort** Sam Houston in San Antonio. Pershing asked **Congress** to allow the Chinese to stay. A 1921 law made them legal immigrants. Later they became U.S. citizens.

Pancho Villa, a Mexican revolutionary, led attacks on Americans in Mexico and the southwestern United States.

The ban against Chinese immigration was lifted in 1943. Large numbers of doctors and professors came to the United States to escape **Communism**. In 1964 Tom. J. Lee of San Antonio became the first Chinese Texan to be elected to the state **House of Representatives**.

Since the 1980s, the Asian population in Houston has grown enormously. New Chinatown on the west side is filled with Chinese shops, restaurants, and grocery stores. Street signs are in both English and Chinese. Apartments advertise free adult English classes. Modern Chinese Texans keep their culture with temples and cultural organizations, Chinese-language newspapers, and festivals. Chinese New Year's celebrations feature dragon dancers and firecrackers.

The dragon dance is an important tradition in China. It is believed to bring luck and happiness, and scare off demons.

Vietnamese, Laotians, and Cambodians

Large numbers of Vietnamese came to Texas in 1975 because of the Vietnam War. Most went to large cities. People fled Laos and Cambodia after the Communist takeover of those countries. Many became shrimp fishers on the Gulf coast where the climate was similar to their homeland.

People of Vietnamese descent feel that a good education is very important.

Many Asians could not speak English when they arrived. Religious groups helped them learn the language and customs so they could find jobs. In the cities, Vietnamese families worked at low-paying jobs until they had money to start their own businesses.

Family is important in Vietnamese culture. At the traditional Vietnamese Mid-Autumn Festival, children receive paper lanterns shaped like animals or stars. They eat moon cakes, which are round rice cakes filled with sweets, sing, and participate in parades. On the Lunar New Year, called Tet, families honor their **ancestors**. They burn both candles and pieces of fancy red paper with messages for their ancestors.

Many Texans

The people of Texas have come from all over the world and brought many of their **customs**, traditions, and heritage to the state. The 2000 **census** showed the **diversity** of Texas and how the state has continued to change today. But no matter where people come from, they are all the people of Texas.

Texas Achievers

Many famous people were either born in Texas or performed important work in the state.

Adair, Christia (1893–1989), **civil rights activist**. Angry after being denied the right to vote because of her race, Christia Adair helped **desegregate** the Houston Public Library, airport, veterans hospital, and city buses. Partly as a result of her work, African Americans became able to serve on juries and be hired for county government jobs. She was one of the first African Americans in Houston to serve as a judge. A county park in Houston was named after her in 1967.

Armstrong, Lance (b. 1971), athlete. Lance Armstrong was born and raised in Plano. A professional triathlete at 16, Armstrong has gone on to become a world-champion bicyclist. He won the Tour de France seven times and was a member of the U.S. Olympic team in 1992 and 1996.

Austin, Moses (1761–1821), pioneer. Moses Austin was born in Connecticut. He moved to the west in 1798 to begin mining for lead. He came to Texas in 1820, and sought permission from the Mexican government to settle 300 American families in Texas. Moses Austin's son, Stephen Fuller, took over the American settlement of Texas after his father's death.

Austin, Stephen Fuller (1793–1836), *empresario*. Stephen F. Austin is often referred to as the "Father of Texas." He was a skillful, patient leader. During the 1820s, he succeeded in bringing 1,200 American families to settle in Mexican Texas. He was imprisoned in Mexico for trying to gain more freedom for Texas. After he returned, the Texas Revolution began, and he went to the United States to gain support for Texas independence from Mexico.

Stephen Fuller Austin

Borden, Gail Jr. (1801–1874), inventor and businessperson. Gail Borden Jr. printed the Texas Declaration of Independence and founded the milk company with his name. When he first came to Texas, Borden raised livestock, **surveyed** land, and eventually started a newspaper. He began inventing in the 1840s. One of his successful inventions was condensed milk. In the 1870s, Borden gave financial aid to Texas schools and churches.

Bowie, James (1796–1836), patriot. Bowie was legendary even before he participated in the Battle of the Alamo. Stories say he killed a man in a **duel** in Louisiana before moving to Texas around 1828. Bowie commanded a group of volunteers who engaged in battles with Mexicans in the fight for Texas independence. He was one of the defenders who lost his life at the Alamo.

Bush, George Herbert Walker (b. 1924), politician. George Bush came to Texas after graduating from Yale University. The Houston oil executive became a member of **Congress**, then vice president before being elected 41st president of the United States in 1988. During his presidency, the Soviet Union broke up, and the **Cold War** ended. When the late Iraqi President Saddam Hussein invaded Kuwait in 1990, Bush worked for the support of the United Nations and sent troops to free Kuwait. The Iraqi army was defeated, and Kuwait was freed. Despite this international success, Bush was defeated in the 1992 presidential election. His presidential library is located at Texas A&M in College Station. A piece of the Berlin Wall, a symbol of **Communism** and the Cold War, is there.

George Herbert Walker Bush (left) and son George W. Bush.

Bush, George Walker (b. 1946), politician. George W. Bush was a Midland oil executive who later became part owner of the Texas Rangers baseball club. He was elected Texas governor in 1994. While governor, he worked with both political parties to pass welfare reform and education programs that stressed reading skills and achievement testing. He left office as governor to become the 43rd president of the United States in 2000. Bush was re-elected to a second term as president in 2004.

Caballo, Juan (ca. 1812–1882), warrior, diplomat, and civil leader. Throughout his life, Juan Caballo served not only the interests of Black Seminoles but also assisted them in numerous **negotiations** with settlers. Caballo became well-known during the Second Seminole War as a negotiator and military leader. During the last two years of the war, he convinced 535 Native Americans to move to **reservations** in Oklahoma.

Cabeza de Vaca, Álvar Núñez (ca. 1490–ca. 1556), explorer. Álvar Núñez Cabeza de Vaca and three companions were the only survivors of a 1528 **expedition** to Florida. After being shipwrecked on the Texas coast, the men spent seven years as slaves of different native tribes. The men escaped and traveled many months before reaching Mexico City. In a book published in 1542, Cabeza de Vaca wrote about the people he met and the things he saw. He was the first to describe the land of North America away from the coastline.

Álvar Núñez Cabeza de Vaca

Cisneros, Henry (b. 1947), politician. In 1981 Henry Cisneros was elected mayor of San Antonio. Cisneros was the first **Hispanic** to serve as mayor of a major United States city. Cisneros served as secretary of housing and **urban** development from 1993 to 1997, under President Clinton. In 1999, Cisneros pleaded guilty of having lied to the FBI in 1993 about secret payments he had made. This **scandal** ruined his reputation and ended his political career. President Clinton **pardoned** him in January 2001.

Coleman, Bessie (1892–1926), aviator. One of 13 children, Bessie Coleman was raised in Waxahachie. She went to an aviation school in France and was the world's first African American to become a licensed pilot. In 1994 the United States Postal Service issued a stamp in her honor.

David Crockett

Crockett, David "Davy" (1786–1836), patriot. David Crockett was born in Tennessee, but he is best remembered as a hero at the Alamo. He was a famous hunter who loved to tell stories. He served in Congress but became disgusted with politics. He and three companions arrived in Texas at the beginning of the Texas Revolution. They rode immediately to the Alamo to participate in the battle for Texas's freedom. Although he was only in the state for three months, Crockett was declared a "Texas treasure" by the legislature.

Eisenhower, Dwight David (1890–1969), general and politician. Dwight D. Eisenhower, general of the United States Army and 34th president of the United States, was born in Denison, Texas. Shortly afterward, his family moved to Kansas. Eisenhower was the supreme **commander** of the Allied Expeditionary Force in World War II, and he gave the order for American and British troops to storm the beaches at Normandy on D-Day, June 6, 1944. As president of the United States, Eisenhower fought to balance the federal budget, construct the Interstate Highway System, and pass the first civil rights law since the Civil War (1861–1865).

Ferguson, Miriam A. "Ma" (1875–1961), politician. Miriam Ferguson was Texas's first female governor and the second female governor in the United States. She was elected after her husband was removed from office for **misconduct**. Miriam Ferguson served two separate terms as governor of Texas, from 1925 to 1927 and 1933 to 1935.

Miriam "Ma" Ferguson

Glidden, Joseph Farwell (1813–1906), businessperson. Joseph Glidden experimented with ways to improve barbed wire. He received a **patent** in 1874 for a machine that added barbs to wire mechanically, making it easier to mass produce barbed wire. Glidden established the Barb Fence Company with his partner, Isaac L. Ellwood. In a few years, barbed wire was being used all over the West. Glidden became one of the richest men in the United States and bought 180,000 acres (72,843 hectares) of land in Texas, where he raised 15,000 head of cattle.

Goodnight, Charles (1836–1929), rancher. Charles Goodnight, a pioneer Panhandle rancher, created a cattle trail from Texas to Wyoming with his friend Oliver Loving. Goodnight invented the chuckwagon for use on cattle drives, and designed the side saddle for his wife. The JA Ranch in Palo Duro Canyon was made by a partnership with Britishman John Adair. Goodnight owned another ranch where he saved bison from **extinction**. He and his wife had no children, but they founded Goodnight College to educate others.

Patillo Higgins

Higgins, Patillo (1863–1955), business-person. Patillo Higgins lost an arm as a young man. He was an amateur **geologist** and was sure that oil and gas existed under the Spindletop salt dome near Beaumont. After several drilling failures, he hired Anthony Lucas, an engineer who eventually found the oil. Higgins went on to drill other wells and deal in real estate.

Hobby, Oveta Culp (1905–1995), businessperson. Born in Killeen, Oveta Culp Hobby was a pioneer for women in the worlds of business and politics. In 1931 she married William P. Hobby, former governor of Texas and publisher of the *Houston Post*. She helped her husband run the Post until 1941. From 1942 to 1945, she served as director of the Women's Army Corps, and was awarded the Distinguished Service Medal. In 1953, she was appointed by President Dwight D. Eisenhower to a **Cabinet** post in the new Department of Health, Education, and Welfare. Hobby was known for her views on race and religion.

Hogg, Ima (1882–1975), art patron and **preservationist**. Ima Hogg was a **philanthropist** who used her wealth to help others. She funded the Houston Child Guidance Center and the Hogg Foundation for Mental Health. A musician herself, she helped found the Houston Symphony. While serving on the Houston school board, she put music programs in the schools and fought for equal pay of teachers, no matter what their race or sex. She also had a large collection of American art and antiques. Because of her knowledge, she **advised** First Lady Jacqueline Kennedy on historic furniture for the White House.

Ima Hogg

Sam Houston

Houston, Sam (1793–1863), politician. Sam Houston played an important part in the founding of Texas. Born in Tennessee, he lived among the Cherokee Indians and learned about their **culture**. Houston fought in the Creek Wars, then studied law and became governor of Tennessee. After his marriage failed, he moved to the Indian Territory. Houston entered Texas at the time of the Texas Revolution. As commander of the Texas forces, he and his men defeated the Mexican army at the Battle of San Jacinto. In 1836 he was elected first president of the Republic of Texas. Later, he married Margaret Lea and served a second term as president. When Texas joined the Union, he spent 13 years in Washington, D.C., as a senator. After returning to Texas, he was elected governor of the state. When the Civil War (1861–1865) broke out, Houston believed so strongly that Texas should stay in the Union that he refused to sign a promise of loyalty to the **Confederacy**. He was removed from office and returned home to Huntsville where he died two years later.

Johnson, Claudia "Lady Bird" (1912–2007), first lady. Nicknamed "Lady Bird" as a child, First Lady Johnson took an active role during the presidency of her husband, Lyndon Baines Johnson. She concentrated on Head Start, a program aimed at helping preschool children from poor families. She also began an **environmental** program, called "beautification," that encouraged people to make their surroundings more attractive. After retiring in Texas, she established the Lady Bird Johnson Wildflower Center in Austin.

Johnson, Lyndon Baines (1908–1973), politician. Lyndon Baines Johnson was born on a ranch near Stonewall. After serving as a member of Congress and as vice president, he was sworn in as 36th president following the **assassination** of John F. Kennedy in 1963. His administration passed civil rights laws and supported the space program. His presidential library at the University of Texas at Austin has a moon rock on display.

Joplin, Scott (ca. 1868–1917), musician. Scott Joplin, the "King of Ragtime" music, was born near Linden, Texas, on November 24, 1868. His ragtime pieces for the piano—including "Maple Leaf Rag" and "The Entertainer"—made him famous. Musicians continued to perform his music for many years after his death. Joplin's music was used in the Academy award-winning movie *The Sting*.

Jordan, Barbara (1936–1996), politician. Barbara Jordan was the first African-American Texas state senator since 1883, and became the first African-American woman from the South to be elected to the United States Congress in 1973. In 1974, she became known for her distinct voice and speeches during the Watergate hearings to **impeach** President Richard Nixon. In 1979 Jordan decided to retire from politics and teach at the University of Texas at Austin. Barbara Jordan was inducted into the National Women's Hall of Fame in 1990 and received the Presidential Medal of Freedom in 1994.

Barbara Jordan

King, Henrietta (1832–1925), businessperson and philanthropist. Henrietta King taught briefly at the Rio Grande Female Institute before marrying Richard King in 1854. The couple lived on a cattle ranch on the Santa Gertrudis Creek, which soon grew to 500,000 acres (202,343 hectares). At the time of Richard King's death, the King Ranch was $500,000 in **debt**. Henrietta King helped the ranch earn money and eventually increased its size to 1,173,000 acres (474,697 hectares), which is larger than the state of Rhode Island. Henrietta King donated land to build the towns of Kingsville and Raymondville, and provided land and money for the construction of churches, schools, and hospitals.

Henrietta King

Lamar, Mirabeau Buonaparte (1798–1859), politician. Mirabeau Lamar, second president of the Republic of Texas, was an excellent horseman who served in the Texas army and later fought in the Mexican War. While president of the Republic, he claimed that Texas extended to the upper reaches of the Rio Grande. Facing conflicts between settlers and Native Americans, he forced most of the tribes to leave. He is known as the "Father of Texas Education" for his efforts in setting aside land for public schools and universities and for encouraging the establishment of a school system. Lamar County and the town of Lamar are named for him.

La Salle, René Robert Cavelier, Sieur de (1643–1687), explorer. In 1684, René Robert Cavelier, Sieur de La Salle sailed to North America to start a French colony near the mouth of the Mississippi River. The ships missed their target and instead landed at Matagorda Bay on the Texas coast on February 20, 1685. Facing starvation, La Salle and his men set out for the **fort** he had built earlier on the upper Mississippi River. La Salle was so disliked that his own men killed him.

René Robert Cavelier, Sieur de La Salle

León, Martín de (1765–1833), *empresario.* Martín de León was the only Mexican *empresario* to found a colony in Texas. His colony, Guadalupe Victoria, was the only colony in Texas with a majority of Mexicans in 1824. Martín de León's cattle carried the first **brand** in Texas. De León was also one of the earliest traildrivers in Texas, driving his herds to market at New Orleans several different times. Martín de León's children later supported the Texas army in the Texas Revolution against Mexico.

Lewis, Carl (b. 1961), athlete. Frederick Carlton Lewis was raised in Houston. During his career as a track-and-field athlete, he earned nine gold medals and one silver medal while participating in the 1984, 1988, 1992, and 1996 Olympic Games.

Michener, James A. (1907–1997), author. James Michener was a famous author who wrote **epics** about places, such as in his novels *Hawaii* and *Texas*. He returned to Austin at the end of his life and donated $19 million for a creative writing program at the University of Texas.

Murphy, Audie L. (1924–1971), soldier and actor. In his lifetime, Audie Murphy earned more medals and honors than any other United States soldier in our country's history. During his World War II career, Murphy received 33 awards, including the Medal of Honor in 1945. He also received honors from France and Belgium. Murphy published *To Hell and Back* in 1949, the story of his experiences in World War II. He acted in numerous movies, becoming one of the world's most popular stars of Western movies. Murphy was buried in Arlington Cemetery, in Washington, D.C., near the Tomb of the Unknown Soldier.

Audie Murphy

O'Connor, Sandra Day (b. 1930), Supreme Court justice. Born in El Paso, Sandra Day O'Connor served as an Arizona assistant attorney general from 1965 to 1969. She entered the Arizona Senate in 1969, and in 1974, she ran successfully for trial judge. She held that position until she was appointed to the Arizona Court of Appeals in 1979. On July 7, 1981, President Ronald Reagan nominated her to the Supreme Court. In September 1981, O'Connor became the Court's 102nd justice and its first female member.

Parker, Quanah (ca. 1845–1911), Comanche chief. Quanah Parker was the son of Peta Nocona and Cynthia Ann Parker, a white woman who had been taken captive as a girl by the Comanche tribe. Parker was the last chief of the Quahadi Comanche. He and his band remained in the Panhandle of Texas after other tribes had been moved to reservations in the Indian Territory. Parker was forced to surrender when U.S. troops captured and killed 1,000 of his horses. On the reservation, Parker led his tribe in adopting white culture.

Quanah Parker

Porter, Katherine Anne (1890–1980), author. Callie Russell Porter was born in Indian Creek, Texas. She wrote under the name Katherine Anne Porter. Her first collection of stories, *Flowering Judas and Other Stories*, established her as a short-story writer. She wrote "Hacienda, a Story of Mexico," "Noon Wine," and *Pale Horse, Pale Rider*, a collection of three short stories. Her novel, *Ship of Fools*, was a best-seller and was adapted into a major film. Porter's *Collected Short Stories* won both a Pulitzer Prize and a National Book Award in 1966.

Porter, William Sidney (1862–1910), author. After moving to Texas as a young man, William Sidney Porter began a career of writing. He worked in bank for a short time as well, and was accused of stealing. While serving time in jail, he wrote short stories, using the name O. Henry. His stories were popular and became well-known. Two of his most famous stories are "The Gift of the Magi" and "The Ransom Red Chief."

Ann Richards

Richards, Ann (1933–2006), politician. Ann Richards was a popular Texas governor who served the state from 1991 to 1995. During her time in office, Richards helped improve Texas's economy. She focused on education and was tough on crime. Richards also appointed many women and minorities to positions in the Texas government.

Rodriguez, Cleto L. (1923–1990), soldier. Cleto Rodriguez fought in the United States Army during World War II (1939–1945) and became an expert shot. While fighting in the Philippines, Rodriguez risked his life during the battle for Manila and showed great courage and skill on several occasions. He later served in the United States Air Force. Rodriguez was the fifth Hispanic person to win the Congressional Medal of Honor.

Sweatt, Heman Marion (1912–1982), civil rights activist. Heman Sweatt was denied entry into the University of Texas School of Law in 1946 because of his race. This began a legal battle over equal higher education for African American students in Texas. After four difficult years in court, Sweatt became the first African American to be admitted to the University of Texas School of Law. Sweatt is also considered responsible for the establishment of Texas State University for Negroes, later renamed Texas Southern University, a college for African Americans that has a law school.

Tower, John Goodwin (1925–1991), politician. John Tower was born in Houston on September 29, 1925. He served in the United States Navy in World War II (1939–1945). Beginning in the 1960s, through the 1980s, Tower served as a U.S. senator for Texas. Tower worked for President Ronald Reagan on important international issues, including talks with the Soviet Union about getting rid of weapons.

Travis, William Barret (1809–1836), patriot. Travis was commander at the Alamo. His famous letter appealing for help is considered a model of heroism.

Lorenzo de Zavala

Zavala, Lorenzo de (1788–1836), politician. Manuel Lorenzo Justiniano de Zavala y Sáenz was the first vice president of the Republic of Texas. Earlier, Zavala participated in the government of Mexico. He was imprisoned for about three years for expressing his **democratic** ideas. During that time he taught himself about medicine and how to speak English. Once General Santa Anna became ruler of Mexico, Zavala gave up his post in the Mexican government. Zavala went to Texas and became a supporter of Texas independence. He helped write the constitution of the Republic of Texas and became its first vice president.

Map of Texas

Capital

City

River

State line

Amarillo
Tulia
Red River
Wichita Falls
Texarkana
Lubbock
Celina
Denton
Fort Worth
Dallas
Marshall
Stamford
Abilene
Tyler
Sabine River
Brazos River
Waxahachie
El Paso
Midland
Odessa
Comanche
Waco
Lufkin
Pecos
Pecos River
San Angelo
Colorado River
Brady
Temple
Mason
College Station
Fredericksburg
Austin
Beaumont
Kerrville
Houston
Alvin
Galveston
Del Rio
San Antonio River
San Antonio
Pearsall
Victoria
Rio Grande
Corpus Christi
Gulf of Mexico
Laredo

McAllen
Brownsville

New Mexico
Oklahoma
Arkansas
Texas
Louisiana
MEXICO
Gulf of Mexico

Glossary

activist someone who publicly supports a cause

advise give advice about something

ancestor one from whom an individual has descended

Anglo having a British background

architect person who designs buildings and gives advice on their construction

assassination murder of an important person by surprise attack

brand mark made by burning with a hot iron to prove ownership

Cabinet group of people who give advice to the president

capitol building in which the legislature meets

Catholic original church of Christianity centered in Rome, Italy

census count of population and the gathering of information about that population

civil rights rights of personal liberty guaranteed by the U.S. Constitution

Cold War competition, tension, and conflict short of actual war between the United States and the Soviet Union

commander person who holds supreme authority

Communism social system in which property and goods are held in common

Confederate person who supported the southern states during the Civil War. The Southern states were called the *Confederacy*.

Congress chief lawmaking group of a nation

culture ideas, skills, arts, and a way of life of a certain people at a certain time

debt money owed to someone

democratic idea that is for the good of all people

descendant group that a person originally comes from

descent to be born of; to come from a given source

discrimination unfair treatment of people based on their difference from others

diverse having variety

duel combat between two persons fought with deadly weapons and with witnesses present

Emancipation Proclamation order issued on Jan. 1, 1863, that freed the slaves of the Confederate states

empresario someone who creates a business, starting with nothing but an idea

environment surrounding conditions that influence the life of plants and animals

epic long tales that tell of a hero's deeds

ethnic belonging to a group with a particular culture

expedition organized journey of a group of people

extinction no longer living on Earth

famine time when food is scarce and people are starving

fort strong building used for defense against enemy attack

geologist scientist who specializes in the history of the earth

heritage something that comes from one's ancestors

Hispanic one of Cuban, Mexican, or Puerto Rican origin

House of Representatives one of two lawmaking bodies of the United States

immigrant one who moves to another country to settle

impeach charge a public official with misconduct in office

industry group of businesses that offer a similar product or service

invest put out money to gain a return

mariachi Mexican street band

metropolitan area surrounding a large city

migrate to move from one place to another for food or to breed

misconduct wrongdoing

mission building that houses a group that sets forth on a task, particularly to spread certain religious views.

negotiate have a discussion with another in order to settle something

pardoned free from penalty or fault for a crime

patent protected by a document that gives an inventor the only right to make, use, and sell the invention for a certain number of years

persecution treat continually in a way meant to be cruel and harmful

philanthropist person who gives generously to help other people

plantation planted area tended to by laborers

preservationist person who protects something historically important from injury, loss, or decay

reservation public land set aside for use by Native Americans

revolutionary person who accomplishes something that no one has done before

rural having to do with the country or farmland

scandal something that causes a feeling of shame

segregate set one type of people apart from others. To *desegregate* means to bring people back together.

sharecropper person who farms another person's land for a share of the crop or profit

survey study a land to determine its boundaries and features

transcontinental extending across a continent

treaty agreement between two parties

urban relating to the city

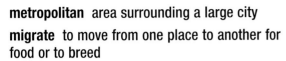

Find Out More

Further Reading

Burgan, Michael. *George W. Bush*. Mankato, MN: Capstone Press, 2004.

Childress, Diana. *George H.W. Bush*. Minneapolis, MN: Twenty-First Century Books, 2007.

Gregson, Susan. *Sam Houston: Texas Hero*. Mankato, MN: Compass Point, 2006.

Haley, James. *Stephen Austin and the Founding of Texas*. New York: Rosen Publishing, 2003.

Website

http://www.texasbeyondhistory.net

This University of Texas at Austin site provides links to explore the entire state (its people, history, culture, regions, and government).

Index